There Are People

OrangeBooks Publication

1st Floor, Rajhans Arcade, Mall Road, Kohka, Bhilai, Chhattisgarh 490020
Website: **www.orangebooks.in**

First Edition, 2025

ISBN: 978-93-6554-215-8

Price: Rs. 299.00

Printed in India

There are People

AASIF SHAH

Orange Books Publication
www.orangebooks.in

For my father, mother and brothers.

Contents

1. Mood

Crows shit on their heads

Crows shit on their cars

Crows shit on their girlfriends

Crows shit on their jobs

Crows shit the dickens of a good Indian.

2. Status Updates

The futility of things absurd has been given a name: love.

Is there a babysitter for loneliness?

He updates. She updates. We try to make out their undying love story.

Plastic plants decorate the sultry air that comes into the grilled window of urban pseudo-ism.

As you keep breathing, you learn more and more and unlearn more and more.

There is destiny. And then there is coincidence.

Becoming somebody is such a big deal nowadays that the other day a mosquito asked me where he should bite me so that I would remember him for the rest of my life.

I love the way my love feels the way, I love the way I love.

If you want to wake up exactly the way you want to wake up every morning, stay single.

3. Cut

Today

Finally

Learnt

How

To cut

Off

My

W

O

R

D

S

4. New Year

Old calendar's down,
New one's up, but nail and wall
Remains the same.

5. Birthday Candles

My birthday candles --

Memories flicker anew

Telling tales of old.

6. Beauty Spreads on Your Face Moment by Moment

Beauty spreads on your face moment by moment

Like a tad full of afternoon sun, dreaming on a taro leaf

Like a cirrus cloud in the sky floating as a motif

Like a bunch of paper lanterns soaring into the night

Like a reflection of the pool blinking on a wall

Like a candle (lone in a room) waiting for light to never come

But your glance grows elsewhere in the party beat by beat.

7. Unshelled

Feelings not hatched into words

Are best dried on your tongue

Like leaves inside a book,

For even if fragile,

Even if they give out the fragrance of the day it was put, which you want

To shout out, sometimes, every bloody time,

Even if they show vicarious flashes stolen in capsules of lost times,

They just want to be taken out before they get glued to the pages

Destroying both themselves and the pages,

For what's the point of getting attached to something that's you-like

Instead of flying free in the wind and landing on something new-like

Growing up -

The places

The spaces -

Growing up -

The reaches

The ends –

Are not the co-ordinates of the moment you are looking for.

An invisible graph that gives stats about your existence

Like the birth of words that we want to eat back -

First the feet,

Then the legs,

Torso, mouth.

Feelings be best kept warmed by our heart,

Guts and darkness.

for who knows when they'd set themselves free

To become a thought, a gesture or a goodbye.

Because once unshelled, unlike us,

They don't want to go back,

They just grow.

8. Ode to a Crow

Is it my fault that I come here and stand?
Waiting for the bus that always comes late?
Or shall I blame you, unknown flying black?
I know your folks. Yet, to name is vain.

All of you look twins to my untrained eyes.
Not a watcher of feathers does help.
Have a song of your own to which I clap?
No, even a season you lack, be damn.

A thing to praise you require extremely.
No bard rhymes of you, poor soul, such a shame.
A life you let with everyman's blame.
And curses, hard and cold, you bear grimly.

A nest but others you visit and stay:
An unsolicited guest sans a bond.
Ah, pigeons are better -- they have their own.
I know too they are your cousins, aren't they?

Say, are you a descendent of Azrael?
Or a distant relative of mitra?
I thing I am really confused, oh gray...
Hey wait, what are you -- gray or black or dual?

What shall I call you -- an angel of death?
There in far eastern land you bring sorrow
To the houses upon whose eaves, you caw.
They fear; they shoo you if you procrastinate.

What shall I call you -- a friendship omen?
There in western land you seem to bring guest
To the house upon whose window you rest.
They hope; they prepare for a gentleman.

What schooling does your sons and daughters do?
I won't bother you for I know not where,
You first raised them. Not to ask I do swear.
How do they follow you? Oh, I undo.

I guess there is nothing they learn these days
Save bombs in the Gulf; in the West War.
And evil in the east; about south, is there?
They play good cricket, or so a fan says.

This morning I woke up and cleaned myself.
Ironed my shirt and pants; studied my gelled hair.
Looked like a dude; the reflection did dare.
A silent mirror said a lot of oneself.

But lo! what you done unto me, oh my,
On my ironed white shirt -- whitest and creamiest,
Making all my hope this morning feel sorry?
Or shall I thank elephants cannot fly?

Will they prosecute me if I drop you
With a missile from a borrowed fork-sling?
Same as the bachelor who went hunting?
A chinkara's death, a murder they blew.

I have a serious doubt: when his speeding car
Ran over four lives, no defence at any!
A miss was killed in front of many
Lacks a witness; guilty is free so far!

World is no better though. Makes you astray.
Go fly away. Thank you. I am so sad.
When you hover over me. If you had
Known singing it would have been another way.

9. Travelling by Bus

Had I been known to her,

Would she stick her knees together?

Those that were open before I took the seat,

What was empty beside her?

I wonder.

10. Message # 9

Do not type the sms yet.
Understand her eyes first.
Keep the caller tune still
Until you study her lips.
Update not the status so soon
Before you master her gestures.
Soft poke stings the most
When one day you wake up
And find her status updated.
For songs become teary
When a game is learnt too late.
But then whose enchanted heart
Has ever been wise?

11. What's Up, New Year?

When cold licks the leaves into curling,
Misty air awakens to lit streets,
Winter warms up with a hot cuppa tea,
A new year, at the edge of a decade,
Waits for an old friend to log out,
I look out the window and recollect.

A friend got engaged to his beloved. nice.
Sometimes love actually happens. really.
Bearded one went back to Kuwait after
Five years of developing friendships here,
and a lover, which in the end ended;
Business is calling him in Dubai.

We head to Byculla for a joint fix,

Churchgate for midnight chit-chat over chai,

Marine Plaza for coffee and a roof.

Some of us are jobless, have no girlfriends,

Some pull hukkah at JJ all night long;

Long hair, nail, bushy beard, smelly armpits.

Ordering pav bhaji at Sukh Sagar from their car, lighting up their classic milds

Is a kick for some, yours truly also.

ayub's is the place for rolls and thumbs up.

Calcutta masala paan at Volga,

Sometimes mitha at Muchchar Paanwala.

Aunty has begun flipping through grooms for

her daughter. She muses her to choose one.

Daughter loves someone who loves someone else.

Society'll talk if you've a love marriage,

Mother explains to her confused daughter.

Practically, the food should be tasty,

Eighty per cent who come to a wedding
Would tell you nonchalantly. forget not.
A brilliant movie maker's been looking
For a producer for three years now with
A strong bound script, a black comedy, but
Producers want commercial stuff with stars.

Drive. Long drive. Drag. Long drag. Talk. Talk progress.
We babble on love, factory, iPhones,
Bbm, marriage, future, money, girls.
It has been two years since we left college,
Nothing has changed, just growing up with eyes
Broad open, learning to live with ideals,

Living in illusion as lost nomads;
Heavy metal blasting in the stereo,
Death grunge in the iPod, banging alone,
Tripping, laughing foolishly, no reason,
Just missing a lover. dark hours. Despair.
We look for work and sensibility,

Among other things, those love and have heartache,
Coming back home, answering to parents,
Feeling guilty for their care and concern,
Taking pills, sleeping for a dream in vain.
Another morning, another feeling.
Useless, shoddy, want to give it up all.

Some have dispersed far away to study,
Friends have parted - got jobs in other states,
Some are picking careers inside a hat.
Should we earn bucks or spirituality?
A new year doesn't make a difference-
We'll kick some more empty cans on the road.

12. Is It What It Is?

Some people run away from love

Some run into it

Some slip upon it

Some write love

Some sing

Some show

Some stand and watch

Some kill

Some die

Some sacrifice

Some dream

Some conquer

Some message

Some talk

Some talk to themselves

Some avoid

Some do not love at all

Some conceal
The wise and the fool do it alike
Who says love is unfair
Love is beautiful
Love is as ugly as it can get
I am hopelessly in love
But who cares
Love is love
Love is not love
You see I love her
No actually, I don't
No no I do
I don't know
Is this love?
Do you always see?
Always feel?
Yeah I know,
I think I know,
I am sure I know,
Wait.
What if?
What is it, anyway?

Is it one way?

Two - way?

Or a circle?

Or a laugh, a cry?

An octagonal confusion?

Draupadi?

Zahera?

Charulata?

What if?

I don't know

Destiny

May be

Take a chance

Or you can pull out your hair bald

Roll on the floor and wish you were dead

Have you moved on?

What is moving on?

How do you move on?

Why not love on?

13. Far Away from You

Far away from you
Enduring the sadness
Longing to be kissed
I bear my sighs

Every phone call
An anticipation
Every message
An expectation

14. If

If Dev Babu were based in Shizu

Where they drink green tea without sugar?

Instead of desi daru or cambodian or rangoon-ish or laos-y

Would he not be more antioxidant than lazy?

Staying fit and young with an activated mind

Not losing any active monies over Chanda

Wouldn't he stop sulking and carry on?

Drinking healthy drinks with his chunni babu

Also, a hara chai without sugar freak

Would he not become a sharp vakil

Fighting cases for Thakur

At which Paro - would not Paro? - unable to

Bear the brunt of being brushed off so

Become a bamboozled bahu rani

Not desired from any direction

Would she not follow her brother-in-law

Till the jaw of Chanda's kotha

There with chanda chit chat

Of here and there, this and that

Gossip to pass her piling time

Of greying hair, wrinkling skin

Man, changes animals, move on

(that kind of talk)

But we women - would not she say? -

We women drink to forget ourselves

Wouldn't she become a zombie

Would not then history be different?

15. Haiku #9

Sure way here to find

My lost unfinished haiku -

She! in my nightmares.

16. Sometimes, I Feel Like Confessing

(Inspired by a poem. Unfortunately, I can't recall its name or its author. Sorry, I didn't mean to. Thank you.)

I get up very late, also later.

i dream more than I write or talk.

I also want to look at attractive faces.

my stomach is not flat, though I climb the stairs.

well, I climb them because the lift's not there.

I want to roam in the middle of the night.

No, I don't want the silence,

I just want to walk.

Good if someone's there, or else it's fine.

I want to scream real loud, sometimes.

I love watching movies all the time.

but Dev.D was not up to the mark.

I should have wanted to become a filmmaker.

I want to fall in love again.

I cry not nor do I sigh, yet I die, sometimes.

I feel I am... no, no, not that.

I want to touch the moon, I can't fly.

I sympathise with animals on the road, Particularly dogs,
I feel like talking to them.

I listen to Kashmir. I relax with comfortably numb.

I want to learn swimming.

I wish I knew dancing.

I wish I knew flattering.

I wish I could overlook lies.

Sometimes I forget names and faces.

Sometimes I forget my tongue and ears.

I want my mobile phone
To learn when to sing.

I want my heart to accept loneliness.
I wish I had a space of my own with a bolted door.
I love my friends, yet
I love to be a black hole, sometimes.

I want to be rude.
I wish I could be rude to some people.
I wish to drive a car when I go to pee.
I want all the people on this earth
To get whatever they ever wanted.
I want to talk to them after that.

I want to fake it all and see.
I want to drink my tears.
I want to take my eyes out
And play roulette with them.
Maybe I could see my future.
I write dreams, fictionalised realities.
Oh yeah, I want to go on a date with the sky.

Is there a Galaxy Mall somewhere?
where stars and planets come out to show off?
I wish I could shop money with my words.
I wish I never knew any money.
I wish I were a gold fish in a bowl
Breathing her love.

Sometimes, I write like this.
Sometimes, I want to get high,
Really high, and write.
Sometimes, sometimes, sometimes.
Sometimes I sleep and wake up
And wish I were sleeping.

Sometimes, I feel like confessing.

17. Some Days Are Like That

You want to roll up your legs and walk on the abuses that are on your mind when

There's a red light that screws your eyes as you look at the red blinks of the meter

But instead tap your fingertips on the red rexin.

In front of your building, you learn how to dribble an imaginary brick

On which you want to land your next step.

Somehow, you realise the elevator is full of inconsiderate souls and red numbers.

When you unlock your door; you miss a beat or two because you had kept the window open.

When you look out the window, you see twisted knots of bamboo creeping up the buildings like Chinese letters.

Then you give the internet wallah as you calm down your annoyed toes on the floor mat that's blushing from repeated rubbing.

You have a hot cup of tea and forget about everything for a while as you munch on the sizzling kanda bhajia, mulling over a certain day when,

As in the film, you walked down the road and sang and danced, and then you smiled because in reality, the distant buildings are still only half seen.

Somethings are not curable just by being drowned in its feel, sometimes you have to say ..., dude.

18. Love Is the Me When I Am Not Myself

Love is the me when I am not myself:
A matchstick that burns and spreads flame,
A muttering charcoal when it dies by itself.

First, it's an illusion; later, an elf.
Circled like a magician's unseen game,
Love is the me when I am not myself.

As if tired, pale and lost, within dark caves
I met closed doors. and restless, I became
A muttering charcoal when it dies by itself.

I dusted the memories from my shelf.
Sadly twisted for there were none to blame.
Love is the me when I am not myself.

I tore up and threw your name down the delph.
But the sea howled to my head's bedlam:
A muttering charcoal when it dies by itself.

In retrospection of my hollowed self,
It was the mad recurrence of your name.
Love is the me when I am not myself:
A muttering charcoal when it dies by itself.

19. For Someone Going Abroad

Pack your bags, my friend. put your dreams in them.
Leave the tears; pass the fears; you won't need them.
Carry happiness in your side pocket.
Take care of the smiles, do not forget.

It's always good to have a smile around.
It lightens things and reflects friendliness.
Be prepared, you will be in a new nest
In a strange land soon. you need smiles profound.

Remember your dreams when you get lonely;
Hang them around your surroundings nicely,
So that every morn you shed your fears
And go about without missing your tears.

Have you put the faith? Good. It comes in handy
When you feel low. always carry your health
In your handbag. check it often, it's wealth.
Take along the language too, spend it for free.

Here, flaunt these badges of our tradition.
Wear a positive feel on your wrist. Have fun.
Keep negativity under your soles
While walking lest it should affect your goals.

Be strong, racism might eve-tease you. ignore.
Fate plays tricks; just make sure you know the rules.
Explore the new freedom. ignite your fuels.
For everything else, leave it to Allah.

20. To A Singing Bird

How many times must you fly across the sea
Before you can see your maturity coming across?
Do you as many times want to be your own boss?
And the blessings you receive, hope you agree.

How many times must you visit the mountain, exploring its mystery, as you wonder at those feelings?
Want to meet other song birds, or are they who you disdain?
The imitating lot sans their own voices or things?

How many times must you sleep in the sand
before you get satiated with the sun and emptiness?
With a decadent happiness, you understand your loneliness.
Suddenly, your breast longs to be caressed by a hand.

How many times must you die inside

Before you know, you need someone to epitomise?

You've seen the world and now realise you too have a life.

To your nest you return and retire with her beside.

21. While watching the Goats the Night Before Eid-Ul-Zuha

Look! how she is having the leaves!
Chewing them slowly but thoroughly,
Taking time in her own measure,
As if she knows how good it is
To nibble on them properly.
She is not alone; she has friends.
And the food is not scarce either--
Many cut branches full of leaves.
She, with nine other companions,
Solemnly shares her last supper.

I witnessed the silent last feast
Being enjoyed at their own leisure
And feel intrigued to realize
That they are waiting for their death.
They will be no more tomorrow.
Are they not brave not to fear death--
Waiting for him in such fashion,
Continuing their day as usual?
How I wish I could talk to her
and ask: How does it feel to know?

22. Memory

Time pushes memory
Off the almirah,
That stores its skeletons,

Like perfect poems
I draft in my dreams
And forget when awake.

23. Hidden Folders

Are these rice leaves put out to dry
Their memories in the morning sunlight?
They reflect the mirages of idle dreams.

You and me, and others,
Came yesterday for the weekend,
To this organic farm with its green fields
Of murmuring impressionism.

Some of these blue plants, the guide says,
Are rare, as things we remember, while
Others are like those we want to remember.

By the river, with your DSLR,
With unnecessary angles,
You want me to flow like it's water
While you capture capsules of me.

I feel like a fishing net in a desert.

When I protest, you lie, I want to upload them.

Upload where? I think of asking,

What about last night?

We didn't capture it on anything.

The sun becomes a fire shower, you forgot your sunscreen.

You can't walk on. we return to our cottage.

You act as if nothing happened

Just so the others don't get curious,

Just so I get curious.

With a smile here and there,

You show me all the memories you've colour-corrected.

I almost took that as if you're ready to forgive me.

We'll leave in the evening
With hidden folders, we can't colour-correct.
Long afterwards, after we've disconnected,
The memories would be liked and commented,
But nobody would know.

24. Cold

My love is the chill you feel
When you skin your ankle
And bear the wound
To the breeze;

It's the sneeze
You didn't sneeze,
The itch near your olfactory mucosa.

Sometimes I see hope,
An epiphany,
Like the dots of white cells
You see, when someone smacks you in the face,

Or like winter in Mumbai
That blinks between December
And January.

25. Love

An old tree longs for company.
A boy comes and waters its
Fragile trunk in his innocence.

He feels good.

'Wish I could help you,' says he to the boy.
'No worries,' comes the reply.

The tree dies.

The boy becomes lonely.
He decides to grow up.

along the way, he falls in love.
But he can't express his feelings.
He is too shy, you see.

One day, the girl gives him a red rose.

'Hi, this is my rebirth as a rose!' says the rose,

'I am the old tree you once helped.'

26. Waiting

I waited as trains passed me by;

trains from Bandra, Andheri, Borivli and beyond.

I waited for a friend, for a promise to be kept,

I was alone among waves of people in a continuum.

I looked at the crows flitting for food.

The smell from the burning stones below,

In a whirlpool with the hot air from the rotating fan above,

Like my thoughts, mixed up in my head,

Because it was past the agreed hour,

as I pretended to be busy with my phone

Whose battery was dead.

The part of the sky that I could see

Through the two opposite serrated roofs,

Seemed to ignore the missing winter.

The sun's on time as you would expect.

The buildings in front of me,
Seen through the fencing hollow,
Stood motionless, one taller
Than the other,
One had a saffron flag,
The other is a green flag,
As if wanting to know, given time,
If they would ever be equal,
Wondering what would happen
If all of them were similar, lengthwise, depth-wise,
(with similar white flags atop),
Like the beds of the railway tracks.

The trains continued,
But no sign of my friend yet.

I heard Maghrib azaan echoing from various corners.
The mikes try to outdo each other's decibels,
Like how debates were drilling my mind:
Was it or was it not today?

Now I was not sure.

Maybe something must have happened.

Or maybe it was not today.

Or maybe I got the wrong station.

Or maybe not.

The trains continued without dropping off my friend.

Then slowly, the people began to disappear.

The crows had flown off, or gone hiding.

The disturbing honk of the trains was heard clearly,

Like the frustration in my mind.

Few people came off the trains. Fewer still got onto them.

But not my friend.

Then the trains stopped.

The dogs started turning up, looking for places to sleep.

I was hungry, tired and irritated.

But just to caress my ego,

Just to feel like it's not a waste of time,

My time,

'At least, after the phone's charged, when I would call my friend,

I would say you did not show up.'

Thinking so, I got up for home, feeling foolish.

27. Corporate Them — Infrastructure

The roads, on my body,

On which my thoughts travel,

They are under construction.

So I use telepathy

For the time being.

28. Crawlers

Some memories are bed bugs
Crawling on your nerves
Itching your peace
Some are lice
Running amok inside your cranium
Some flash string
As if a toe hair is pulled off unannounced
What do you do when they
Creep up while you're trying to sleep?
You toss everywhere on your bed
Till they pass away like a catfish dies
After repeated blows to the head.

29. How To Answer Your Paper

I went there

Half an hour late

Sat and turned my neck 360 degrees

Saw some familiar eyes

"Oh yeah," My eyes greeted them,

And then saw some taking extras

"How can you, nerds?" I wanted to scream

Took a close look at my question paper

Some words I understood

I studied the whole two pages

I took time to study

I was trying to understand

It was an effort

I undressed my pen

And licked it all over

Molested it with my fingers

I caressed the papers

Both the typed and the blank

I was

Fondling

While thinking

With dull steps

He came

I signed

And he signed

I resumed thinking

I looked up again

Too many make-outs

Among pens, papers and fingers

I saw strange blissfulness

I saw sad faces

I saw some hidden teeth

Cleavages

Silhouetted bras

Disturbed hair

Forbidden cells

And useless power specs
Sunlight sneaked in
I missed my sleep
Then I thought
"What the ...?
What exactly is the purpose of all this?
Why can't this be optional?"

Maybe those who
Drafted the policy
Knew something I didn't
Maybe they have some reasons
In their ancient, rigid brains
Oh, let it be
Why care?

I stopped thinking
I stopped everything
I was bored
Then I started
With extreme seriousness
writing on the answer sheet

I wrote my name
Roll number, subject, date
And the language in which
I was supposed to write
I was done
I was happy
Now they'd know
I too was here
I got up
Submitted the paper
And I left.

30. Love And I

i

Why look for pain in others' lines, Aasif?
You have your lines, your pain -

Love sees me the way
The cat sees a dog

Love avoids me the way
Mosquitoes avoid all-out

Love is not my cuppa
But cuppa is my love

Love doesn't have my phone number
Nor does my phone have any lover's number

Love is all night up without a wink
The way sound sleep is without dreams

Love is heaven's key
Hell has no locks

Love does not owe me
Nor do I borrow

Love is surprised when I appear
The way a bat is while hitting a wall

Love dresses well
I follow no trend

Love is spring
I am not a leaf

Love does not gesture
Nor do I stop at signals

Love is calm

I am restless

Love loves love

I love someone

Love plays games

I prefer watching them

ii

Love just happens

I am just but only

Love is deep

I can't swim

Love dreams

I am an insomniac

Love connects

I am a loner

Love is a song

I am not a singer

Love is divine

I am human

Love forgives

I am forgetful

Love is in the air

I don't have wings

Love is a clear blue sky

My moods are cloudy

Love tingles

I am single

Love is love

I am me.

31. My Dreams

I woke up and found my dreams rusted.
I decided to sell them off in the market.
I became a salesman: seller of dreams.

People were amused and nonplussed.
How can you sell a dream? They asked.
I explained, always with a smile.

So, they came in droves to see my stall.
New things are attractive, they said.
But they never bought my dreams.

There's another stall across the road.
The guy there sold money -- sold a lot.
He had old and regular customers.

He was fat, bald and grim.
Yet people smiled at him.
I found out his modus operandi.

He bought money and sold it.
It was like a child's game.
Anybody could do it.

Here I was trying to sell people
Morality, honesty, and principle.
I wanted them to be happy and content.

But they wouldn't listen to me.
They drifted towards the fat pygmy.
They laughed at me sometimes.

I wouldn't understand at all.
How can they, in his trap, fall-
Buy money and be happy?

Did I make a mistake?
My dreams were at stake.
The sun was hotter.

I became tired of explaining.
That's when she came dashing.
She came with her friends.

They examined my stuff
With a serious bluff.
And she started commenting on them.

I tried my best to charm her.
I tried to be a master seller.
I told her how my dreams were different.

But she just said things societal:
This one is lofty, not practical.
Don't be selfish. think about others.

For a few days, she came daily.
I waited for her eagerly.
I began to have a lover's folly.

How will this help me?
This and that, continued she.
Her friends joined in the merry.

I saw the futility of pursuing her.
I gave up my business venture.
I told her to leave my dreams alone.

I began to love my dreams more.
I saw them differently from before.

One fine evening, I closed down my stall.

I put my dreams in the bags and
Brought them home once again.
Then I cried.

32. Tonight I Will Have My Last Despair

My love

The one I loved

I have loved you

Sometimes I have loved you

I have imagined

You in my arms

And wondered

Of the bliss

I have taken you

To mountains

And felt

The innocence

I sat
Opposite you
And listened
And thought
Of things
You never said

I have watched movies with you
And had the pop corns
While the movies ran

I have tasted the coffees
And contemplated dreams
That were never realized

I have drenched
In the rain
With you by my side
And admired
Are lips that never smiled for me

I have proposed
To you in front of my mirror
Which never appreciated

I have talked to silence
At times when i saw
Your shadows

I have messaged you
Texts that I thought
Would make you laugh
And laugh you did
But never understood

I have called you
And told you stories
About other people
For i thought
That would interest you
Interested you were but
Never in me

I have changed myself
And you have changed me
But the change
Didn't occur
Where it should

I have waited for your eyes
And you have always looked at me
But never at my heart

I have had joyful moments
With you and you alone
And I regret
To turn, them to pain

I have tried to burn them
But burned my fingers instead

I wrote you
When I remembered you
What I thought of you
How I intensely loved you

Yes you must be there
thinking over words
which are not mine
your ears were never mine
It was just that
I loved you

Maybe I love you still

But not tonight
Tonight I will have the last despair
The time, you will take to read this
Will be the last time
We will be spending together
And this line will be the last line
You will ever read from me
Which is meant for you.

33. Your Photos Look at Me

The way you always were

These photos are flowers now

Growing younger on my eyes

Photosynthesising my aches

Their roots creep along my veins.

34. I Love You But...

Some women say I Love You the way they adjust their bras:

Freely when they are alone but subtly when they are not.

Some men say it the way they flick ash off their cigarette:

Out of necessity but with style in a disdainful manner.

Some women say it is the way they wear a wristwatch:

They know they can take it off any time they want.

Some men hide it as if they are hiding a hard-on:

however hard they may try, it still stays obvious.

Some women say it's the way they pin curls on their hair:

for a purpose that's different from the real expected one.

Some men say it's the way they play poker;

Revealing nothing yet with a desire to win.

Would that not it be easier if they just said I Hate You?

35. Song

i

As I travel along the highway
and see the open fields,
I miss home.

The bus moves fast,
Leaving them after
Just a glance.

There, far away in the east,
The same stalks
Must be sweet - smelling:

The fresh stalks that remain
After the hay has been cut
Like tough children.

Their fragrance teases me
Nostrils with a sultriness.
The grain long harvested.

Like, in this northern land,
They glitter in front of
My misty eyes.

ii

The open-ness, golden yellow,
Looks bright and crispy.
Yes, everything is crispy in April.

Ah, once he had said,
"April is the cruellest of all."
How true!

How unfortunate!
I see no lilacs.
Or would it make a difference?

Should I see them
To believe, what he had said.
Or is it enough?

Dry and dead leaves
Dance in the air
As they descend in harmony.

iii

If it were October
The yellow'd be brighter
And birds would be merry-making.

While the funny man
They erect to protect,
Stands with arms stretched.

A straw man, he is
With real but torn clothes;
A smile - a curve drawn.

The hat is broad.
The eyes, lips, and nose:
An art; aye, it looks scary!

A season they wait
For their grand feast
And each other's company.

How truly beautiful!
If only we imitate them.
Alas, we do not share our food.

iv

The road is straight and long.
With tall trees on either side
Affecting incomplete shades.

But who cares?
Is the hot air
A little in wanting?

As the vehicle wants to fly,
Our faces are kissed
By the humid wind.

Brakes here and there:
People have to get in and
Get off.

The conductor seems busy
Struggling through the people
That crowd and choke.

It's stuffy inside this already
Full, small box of tin.
It must be the same over there.

Buses are the same everywhere,
always.
Old, grunting yet overburdened.

V

Now again my vision
Upon the vast space.
The wires are the same.

So are their towers.
And the buffaloes?
No, we have cows in our fields.

Were it harvesting time
Men and women I would see
With towels around their heads.

Bending over the grains,
Sickles in hands, singing,
While sweat bathe their bodies,

Making bundles of hay
That would scatter across the
Fields. when they dry...

I remember, we used to play
Upon them, it was fun.
I wish it were not gone.

vi

A treat to the eyes
The scene that will be
When these fields bloom again.

A mind will refresh.
An idea will appear;
Which, if not taken, is lost forever.

But that time is not now.
It's a summer away.
Yet the images are vivid.

Ah, I can't help
But remember all this.
And make myself envy.

That time'll come again.

But mine has gone.

A memory lingers.

A childhood lost,

An adolescence bewildered

And now a man?

vii

The wind blows.

The trees bend in protest

As if disturbed.

But their leaves in waves

Dance to the tune.

Oh, happy trees!

At the point where,

The spreading meets the horizon,

I see darker trees.

But miss something:
Oh, mountains-
Mountains and hills and plateaus!

They're plenty in our land.
Anywhere your head turns
You'll see them talking to the sky.

The sun too would have risen
from behind them.
And a bit cooler too.

All this makes me feel...
Or is it just an imagination?
After all, it's April everywhere.

36. Happiness Is

Happiness is

To find sunlight

On my window

When I wake up

In winter

To have hot chai

As I read newspapers

Some name flashing

On my cell screen

Finding my queue

Diminishing

Finding loose change

In my pocket

At a metro

Token counter

To get a seat

In a packed hall

Finding green lights
When in a hurry
To laugh myself
When getting up
After a fall
To have best friends
Who also laughs
To dream about
Beautiful girls
Able to talk freely
To hum unseen
To shake, stepless
To dream fearlessly
To gossip
On common hatreds
Meeting surprises
Being in love
And being loved
Finding crumpled
Notes in old jeans
Opening albums
And relishing
Captured moments

Writing without

Unsure commas

Able to sleep

Sound and deep

But certainly

Not a toothache.

37. There Are People

There are people
Who Know what heartbreak is
To love and not be loved back
The meaning of simplicity
How to smile freely
How to flee from despair
The address of the nearest post office
What it's like in Delhi
To walk down the roads in summer
What it's like to find a dustbin at metro stations
How to look at the trees
That stand as statues
Not to stretch any ear
For a singing bird
The exact time to open the tap
The number of every bus
How to bargain with auto wallahs

What to do when stuck in a traffic jam
There are roads under construction
There are unfinished metro tracks
And flyovers
The meaning of Delhi Jal Board
How to beg at red lights
How to sleep on pavements
How to shit on pavements
How to sell smacks on pavements
How to sell coconuts
How to occupy a lady's seat
How to spit on the road
How to pee anywhere
How to brave from those apathetic eyes
Hidden behind big, black glasses
How to swallow abusive words
How to go without food
How to abuse each other
What policemen do
What goes on inside ac cars
What it's like to be raped
What is blood, death and mercilessness
How to live below other fellow humans

How to somersault between vehicles

How to jump off a bus when the conductor comes

How to remain obstinate when being chastised,

And there are people who don't.

First published in Pothiz, August 2010.

38. Their Hobby

As I look out of my window
I see an old Gul Mohor tree
Upon whose bough sits a sparrow,
All alone, although quite happy.

The tree is dressed anew in green
Clothes brought by the spring as a gift.
Spring gives hope wherever it's been
Before moving away soon in a drift.

Hey, look! our bird's got company.
A friend arrived with the slow breeze
That fluttering leaves twice too many.
By their pleasantries, they look pleased.

The friend turns toward my window
And holds me with her tiny eyes.
I stare at her, glad that she saw.
And slowly we exchange our smiles.

The other chirps flirtatiously;
Tries to attract my attention,
Which I oblige mischievously,
Much to the friend's irritation.

We're enjoying our game profoundly,
When suddenly a stone flashes
And hits her She falls on the ground.
With a jerk, she dies motionless.

Her friend flies away, terrorized,
After shedding quick, mournful tears,
Scared that she might get the same prize.
The branch becomes empty with fears.

I rush down fast with my heart sad.
There are three boys, each with a slingshot,
Surround the lifeless divine pet,
Ready to claim her at the spot.

It is our hobby, they all say.
I shoo them off, telling them it's bad.
With my pen, I dig up the clay;
Pray, and bury my beloved.

39. I Take a Broom and Sweep My Room

I take a broom and sweep my room-
A small act but a healthy pact.
It keeps a place pure and prevents
Rats, coughs, itches and laziness.

It sweats the tissues of the face,
Arms, legs, chest, hip and posterior.
It agitates the brain afresh,
Excites the eyes, nostrils reflex.

Curl of this bundled coir tickles
Every limb of furniture,
As it travels, thrashing stubborn
Specks of cobweb that cling to them,

Like fibres stuck 'tween the molars
After a meal of a mutton dish,
Or taming the fluffy feather
That often seems to fly away.

Kith and kin of paper, sand, hair,
Grain and unknown aliens gather
Like a lil hill in a corner.
The picker feeds them to the bin.

The floor glitters like a mirror.
Few dust molecules prance proudly
In the warm sunlight which comes bright
Through my window's willing welcome.1

40. Marble Stories

Marbles and my childhood,
The world and my brothers,
Innocent pride and laughter -
Everything was good then.

Dad bought me pouches of marbles.
I lost them all and cried.
Sweets and coins were bartered with them.
Some people would give me one or two.
With ached joy, I would take my aim.

My head was big.
Big heads hit many: naive philosophy.
Heads and holds were varied,
As varied as our cunning.

Cousin of mine, was the king.
He could hit any shot with a wily flick.
His jingling pockets were our envy.
What are you doing with the boys?' Uncle would shout
Also my cousin. she would not listen.
Her fingers were a target's nightmare.
Her head was green and clear.
Green is lucky, she would blink.
We would believe.

When mother would deny us to play at home,
We would simply go to Grandma's place.
Our friends' places were the last options.

During vacations, we would gather on the clay
And dirty our fingers till magrib azaan
Would bring our mothers with fire on their chappals.

We would go to school with marbles in our bags.
The recession was awaited while chewing bubble gum.
Division was taught; perfect shots were learned.

Tak! Hit the marble!
The joy was more than our marks.

We endured our teachers' canes.
Those trees in our school compound
Would lament our teachers' destruction;
Small branches were plucked off to bite our hands.

When I won too many,
I would have sweet dreams.

We also played in groups.
Loud southerners were always ready to fight.
Soft easterners lost most of the time.
Westerners played away only when
The temptation was good.

We, the northerners, were gypsies.
We feared none. We had our money.

Elders would join us sometimes.
When they ran out of marbles,

They would steal one or two from the board
While we dropped our heads on the line.

The head, which stays on the line
Is first, and then nearer the line
Goes second and so on.
If you hit someone else's head, you go last.
That was the religion.

How I once bit my cousin
Because he would not return my marble.
Mother said, But he's won it."
How I doubted his generosity.

During the day, friendships were strategically formed
According to marbles ‘shared or not shared.
And in the night, we all would have dinner together.

Those were the days.

41. To A Silent Spectator

Lend me a voice, give me a choice.
Do not give in to being scared,
Scared of camouflaged special acts.
Tell me to go back,
Shoo me off to somewhere else.
Throw me out with words, with words.

Seven hills speak but my tongue.
Think of me as tired. do me a favour:
Let the hills echo not my outings,
Let the flowers decorate not my mistakes,
Let the rivers carry not my doings,
Let the fields not grow off my remains,
Let the children learn to duck and crawl on the ground,
Or inch under the bed, at the sound of crackers
They themselves lit up,

Let a mother, and all mothers, not be afraid
When you don't return home at night,
Let her not shudder at every passing truck
Thinking of white sheets that's no longer white.

I am not a solution, I am not the solution.
speak up, you, otherwise I am just a stray bullet,
I have no power to stop by myself.

42. Stars

Like

Mirrors stitched on sky fabric

Eyes of fish on surface water

Waves of serotonin

Across a silent night

A mind newly in love again

Child's heartfelt laughter

They open and close their eyes

Emitting remains of milk teeth

Glinting trees of summer

Bunches of smiling leaves

Polka dots of miniature moons

First kiss of a new lover

That blooms cirrus clouds

Goodbye, stubborn Deja Vu

And hello sunrise

They flicker on.

43. Silence

I like the sound of midnight

It reminds me of her heart

That didn't beat for me.

44. Rain

I wanted to write

But you popped up in my mind

A cloudburst happened.

45. Longing

Disco lights blink in the endless sky

They are breath taking

But I miss the halogen bulb.

46. Earthquake

Furniture in my room howled

My bed sprung me up

Then stillness, but my heart didn't.

47. Heartbreak

I stole a quick glance

You were laughing at your phone

Foolish! I turned back.

48. Rainbow

Tiny concurrent arcs appear

Across the semi- circular sky

Click! Sound of my phone camera.

49. Lunar Eclipse

Behind the hills hid the moon

A reddish knife cut her in half

Blood splashed across the darkness.

50. Love

When I fell in love

The gravitational waves were produced

Twisted my goldilocks zone.

51. Unrequited Love

I check her stories

A storm brews; a rain pours out

Whoosh! A phone flies off.

52. Song

We are perfect with our perfect flaws

The memories we have are not all ours

We encounter pieces of our first love

In people we meet, in songs we hear, in perfumes we pass by.

53. Ecosystem

I am part me, part you
fathers, mothers,
clothed, naked
hunger, cloyed
A glass of water, rivers
chicken, potato
roads, destinations
fields, hills
sky, earth
time, memory.

54. Snap

I snap at words, conversations,
Emotions, connections not formed yet
It's not intentional, but
At times I want to undo. No point though
For wonderful futures, moments,
Strangers becoming known,
Friends thinking of me, smug,
It would have been the same.

55. Goan Beach

The sea reflected the movements of stars

She had a yellow tribal art crop top, red dotted, Pyjamas, hair braided at the bottom

Had a shell necklace that slept on the contour of her breasts, her small breasts

I couldn't see her feet, maybe buried in the sand, her eyes like fireflies

As her buzz flared as she sucked at the other end

I looked at her, she looked at the stars

Isn't it beautiful, the stars - she exhaled

Did you know they are their pasts, not there anymore, where we see them now

An illusion of sorts

Like our memories

Each dot a memory of ours?

I didn't

What about the shooting stars?

Those were our regrets - she passed me the buzz

I looked at my memories

I could trace my constellations

My brightest star

My Milky Way

Showers of shooting stars

I inhaled

I didn't believe her, but she seemed kind.

56. Reminiscence

Have you been to a coffee shop lately
Spilling those canteen days
Where you wanted to change the world
But sang songs, gossiped, and laughed instead
Bunked classes sat by the sea
Curly smoke, curly clouds, curly heartbreaks
That senseless anxiety about everything.

Have you been into one of those torn, unwashed jeans
Meeting old times hidden in its pockets
Roads that led to parties, police stations
Those cheers to heart's content
While being broke too often
Those fights with parents
And leaving the house
Not knowing where not giving a damn

Have you been into a photo on Facebook

And wondered about those unplanned loves

Missed those cancelled trips

Those haunting memories

Those albums, that one picture

Have you been thinking about time?

How utterly magnificent you were

How now there's your alarm ringing

Your coffee machines, ironed pants, and routines and routines and routines.

57. Our Now-Moment

While our pasts talk,

Let's not worry about 'ifs'.

They may get along,

With some similarity, with some puzzle.

they may reveal secrets in turn, or not.

Let's not stir the words or smiles

That are around us,

Let's hang out with our now moment

Without any yesterdays or morrows.

Someday our pasts might stop

Being curious about themselves,

Or about us, time may fall off,

This moment is ours now, if not given attention,

May become silent, vanish forever.
Also let's not forget
That if too attached
It tears off a part of you and a part of me
Like a leaf would when it's pulled off
From the pages it got stuck between.

58. Déjà vu

Love doesn't rest in our hearts
Like dew after a night of rain
But in our scars
Like embers of stars at dawn.

59. Love

1

She and i break up all the time.

She is a pendulum that goes-- never again to forever hers.

And I am a boomerang that flies away, that comes back.

Sometimes she blocks me,

Sometimes I do not return her calls.

2

But the beauty of our break-ups,

Like an appetite after a fever,

Like an ice on aching muscles,

Is the jigsaw formed by our broken pieces

I/she loves me/her,

She/I possess her/me

More than we have ever broken up.

60. Spell

She has a black heart,

She makes kajal out of it.

Which spreads on her eyes,

And her eyes become black holes,

And my space is distorted.

61. These Days

These days, you keep coming up in me
Like waking up many times during sleep
Like a cloudburst while too much sun

Now you pop up weird, untamed, beautiful
In my silence during conversations
While folding up breath taking hills

You laughed, looking at me
Like a full - bloomed sunflower
Your eyes spreading like smiles
And I pretended it's nothing

I've started taking screenshots
Of these ephemeral explosions
That's rattling my heart these days.

62. You

You are walking
One small black shoe after
The other as if it doesn't want to
Walk an ebb if you have to
I want you to walk in happiness

From a distant sunlight
Like a vanilla ice cream
Your face hides nothing
A galaxy of longings

You are nearer now, a bit taller than
I thought, still small hands
You have dusky eyes
Wide red lipsticked smiles

You smile like waterfalls
Squinting your eyes like raindrops
I want you to smile with happiness

I watch you go into the building
On the top floor of which I am standing
Rewinding what I just saw
Keep going into my heart
You light up my dark rooms.

63. Don't Love Me A Cliché

Love me like an untamed flood
That can't be garlanded with bands
That breaks hardened soils and spirits
Like an intense earthquake
That stirs nights out of nowhere
That wakes up innermost secrets
Like a blinding summer noon
That pricks our limbs, our face
That breaks our desires black
Like a roaring storm
Where our roots are torn off
Where broken pieces float in ecstasy
Smash me with your mood swings
Crush me between your smiles
Itch me with your syllables
Whirl me in our eyes.

64. Armed Forces Special Poems Act

I'll kill you if you don't like my poem.
I'll shoot you if I suspect you laugh,
I'll arrest you if your cell phone rings,
I'll search you if you flicker your eyes,
I'll rape you if you get up to go,
And if you go, I'll do a combing
Operation to torture your folks.

Don't say these words are wrong,
These words need no warrants,
Don't stand up for what's right.

First published in Narrow Road Volume 2, August 2017.

65. Howling Mothers

The street posts weep
To the beats of stones
In our mothers' hands.

Stones picked up
From bloody roads,
Beat the posts
Waking us to our protection
From viciousness.

Mothers, young and old, shout
Through the night to protest, to protect,
Carrying bamboo fire in their hands,
Against viciousness.

Fire carries their dead
On the burning wicks
Those are torn from their phaneks,
On holders made of their bones.

Fire explodes in their veins
To stop dark special powers,
That comes knocking on doors,
Unwarranted, from taking away
Moons and stars at muzzle point.

Fire vibrates to the rhythm
Of the spirits of those missing,
Looking for dying, dead, vanished offspring,
Justice, equality, and peace.

Howling mothers will march,
All through the night, forever,
Looking out for danger
Of viciousness.

66. *Summer*

I want to write a poem
Of dark trees
Lines of feeling
Green leaves
Mangoes

Of love, smiles, holding hands
Heartaches
Of the first kiss
Haunting images
Ice creams

Of
Rains
Road smells
Drenched hair
Tears

Of

You

Your eyes

Your breasts

Your goodbye.

The End